T05

LIBRARY
ANDERSON ELEMENTARY SCHOOL

W9-BHL-174

superstars!
superstars!
superstars!
superstars!

CREATIVE EDUCATION SPORTS SUPERSTARS

105 LIBRARY
ANDERSON ELEMENTARY SCHOOL

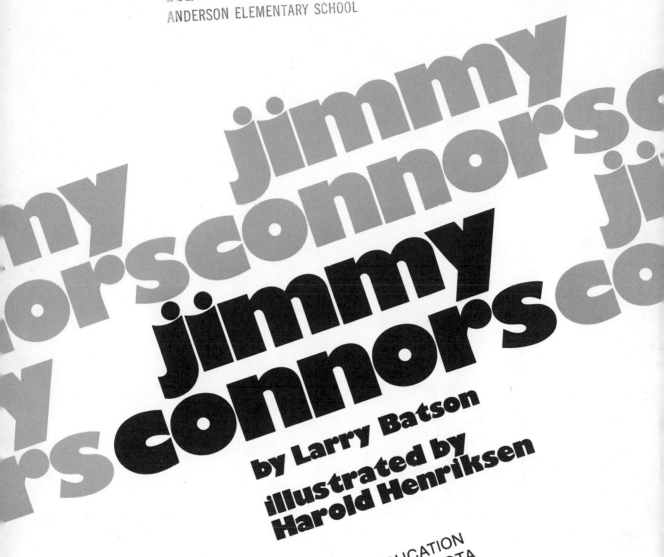

jimmy connors

by Larry Batson

illustrated by
Harold Henriksen

CREATIVE EDUCATION
MANKATO, MINNESOTA

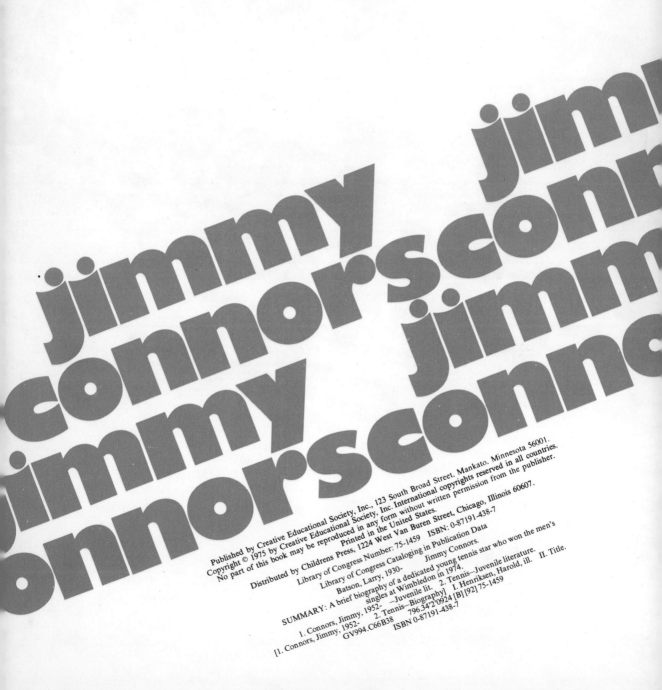

Published by Creative Educational Society, Inc., 123 South Broad Street, Mankato, Minnesota 56001.
Copyright © 1975 by Creative Educational Society, Inc. International copyrights reserved in all countries.
No part of this book may be reproduced in any form without written permission from the publisher.
Printed in the United States.
Distributed by Childrens Press, 1224 West Van Buren Street, Chicago, Illinois 60607.
Library of Congress Number: 75-1459   ISBN: 0-87191-438-7

Library of Congress Cataloging in Publication Data
Batson, Larry, 1930-   Jimmy Connors.
SUMMARY: A brief biography of a dedicated young tennis star who won the men's
singles at Wimbledon in 1974.
1. Connors, Jimmy, 1952-   —Juvenile lit.   2. Tennis—Biography.
[1. Connors, Jimmy, 1952-   2. Tennis—Juvenile literature.   I. Henriksen, Harold, ill.   II. Title.
GV994.C66B38   796.34'2'0924 [B] [92] 75-1459
ISBN 0-87191-438-7

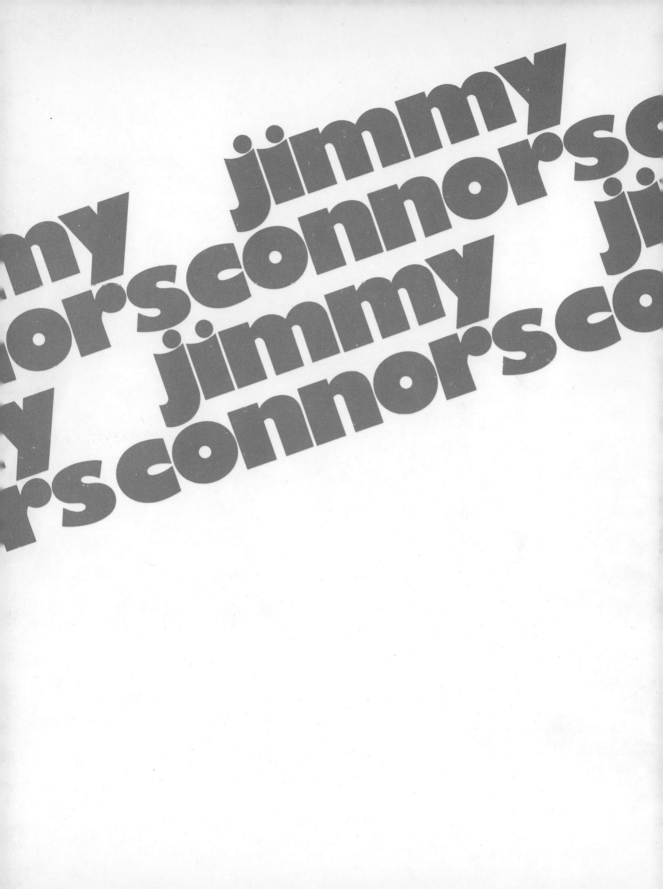

Jimmy Connors is a giant-killer in the world of tennis. He is younger, smaller and less powerful than most of the players he meets. But he is quick and determined and tireless.

On the court, Connors attacks furiously. He throws himself through the air to make returns other players call impossible. He tries to hit every shot on the run, putting the weight of his body and his own momentum behind the racket.

During a match, Connors's mop of brown hair flops wildly as he rushes the net or darts left and right. His cheeks and nose turn bright red from exertion. He grins and frowns or makes faces of surprise and disgust. At the end of a match, he is likely, if he has won, to hurl his racket high in the air and whoop with joy.

At times like that, Jimmy Connors looks like a happy boy who has wandered onto the wrong tennis court. For men's tennis, the professional game, is a game of power.

The world stars are mostly men of above-average height, better than 6 feet. They are very strong with long, stringy muscles and can swing a racket so fast that it blurs. They can serve a tennis ball so swiftly that it is difficult to follow with the eye — up to 148 miles an hour, according to scientific tests. They can hit a return shot hard enough to knock the racket spinning from the hand of an ordinary player.

Connors is barely 5-feet, 10-inches tall and weighs 155 pounds — sometimes 7 or 8 pounds less than that after a long, hard match. He is surprisingly strong for a person of his size, but he cannot play the "power game" type of tennis for very long periods. He can smash a few serves during a match as hard as some of the other top players, but only a few. The rest of the time, he must rely on quickness and skill and strategy.

There is one other important ingredient in Connors' success. It is determination. He is a ferocious competitor who plays every shot as if it were the deciding one. He concentrates so hard during a match that sometimes he forgets the score or even who he is playing.

Most tennis stars develop slowly and steadily. They play first in tournaments for young people and gradually move into the tougher adult competition. Usually the older players know all about the promising young ones.

But Jimmy Connors burst upon the world of tennis like a bomb. He was still a teenager when he turned professional in 1972 — a 19-year-old lefthander who seemed to be able to return any serve. Connors drove two-fisted backhand shots to the baseline then charged the net to put away the return shot if there was one.

Connors won $90,000 in prize money that first year.

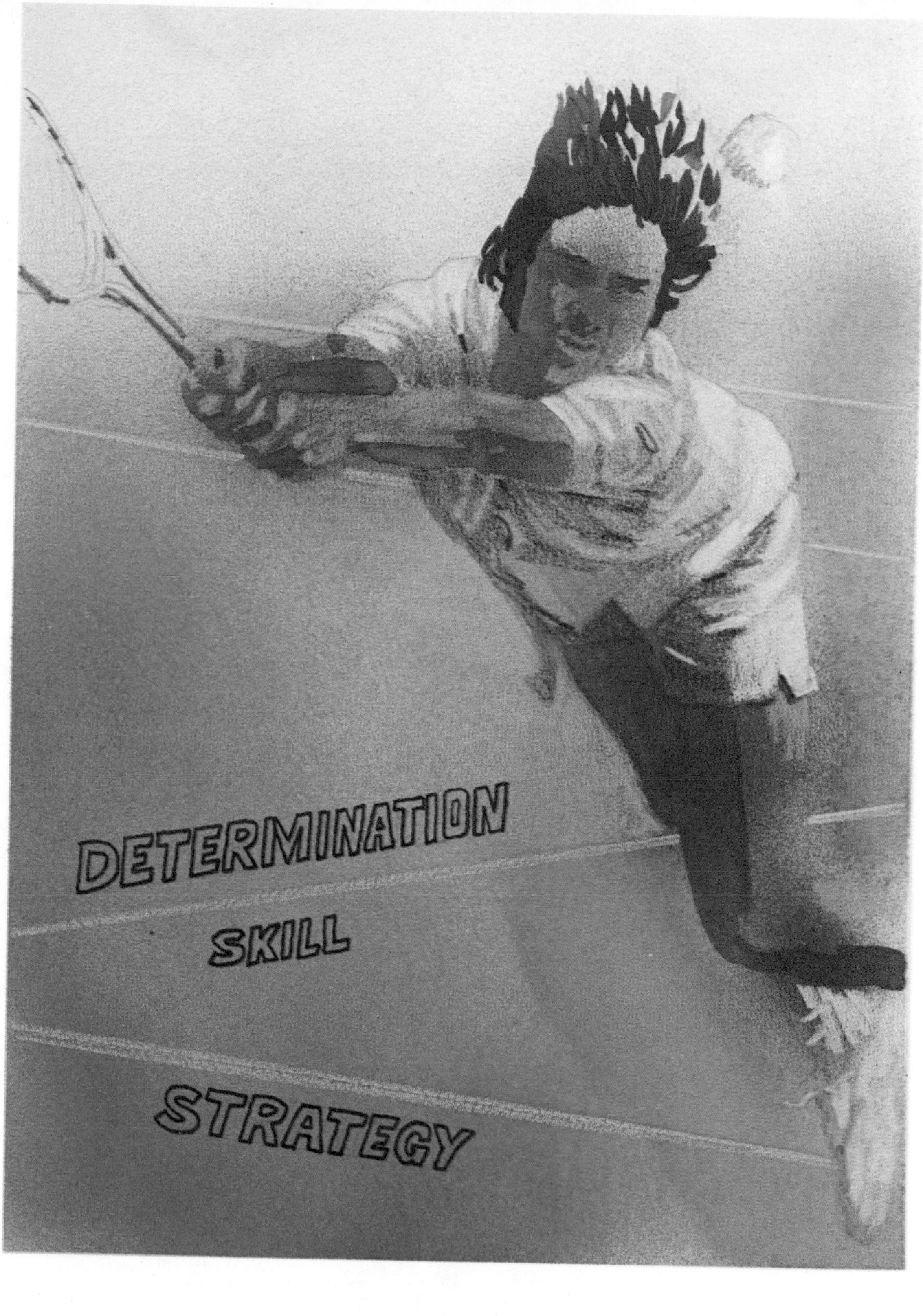
DETERMINATION
SKILL
STRATEGY

Two years later he was earning at least three times that amount and had established himself as the foremost male tennis star in the world.

To understand Jimmy Connors, to know how much tennis has meant to him and how he has achieved so much at such a young age, you have to go back to his earliest childhood.

He was born September 2, 1952, in East St. Louis, Illinois, a city on the Mississippi River across from St. Louis, Missouri.

Jimmy's father, James, operates a bridge across the river at Belleville, Illinois, a span that must be opened for barges and other river traffic. His mother, Gloria, and his grandmother, Mrs. Bertha Thompson, were both good tennis players who gave lessons.

Jimmy first picked up a racket at age two. He swung — two-fisted, of course — at a ball bounced to him by his grandmother, whom he called "Two-Mom." Jimmy never wanted to be anything but a great tennis player.

"Tennis is my choice, my life," he told interviewers later. "I never had time for anything else. I used to leave school at noon to practice."

"Mom" and "Two-Mom" encouraged Jimmy to play but they never let him wear himself out. He was always eager for more. As he grew older, it became obvious to the women that he could be a star because of his quick reactions and his dedication.

The strongest part of Jimmy's game is his ability to return serves. He sweeps into the ball just as it rises from the court, almost appearing to scoop it off the surface. Most players can't react that fast. They have to wait until the ball has risen higher or even reached its peak after hitting the court. That gives the person who served more time to rush the net and get into position to smash the return out of reach.

Jimmy developed his style from the very beginning on the wooden floor of an old armory in St. Louis where his mother gave lessons. The floor was also used for dances and military drills and it was slick, uneven, and treacherous. Jimmy had to hit serves quickly before they could spin away.

Jimmy's brother, John, 18 months older, played with him in those years. Jimmy says that John could have been as good a player as he, but that he lacked the dedication that kept Jimmy practicing for hours every day. John enjoyed dating and all of the things that teenagers normally do. Jimmy just played tennis. "I didn't even know anybody in school," he has said.

When Jimmy was 16 it became obvious that he needed more expert teaching and tougher competition. If

Teacher

Tennis is a game of

STRATEGY

he didn't get it, he would never reach his potential. His mother asked an old friend, Pancho Segura, once a touring professional and now one of the finest teachers in tennis, to take over Jimmy's instruction. Segura agreed and Jimmy, his mother, and grandmother moved to Los Angeles. His father remained in Illinois where his job was.

Jimmy played against the many young tennis stars in Southern California and studied under Segura, twice a national amateur champion, and Pancho Gonzales, one of the all-time great professionals.

After practice Jimmy would sit for hours with Segura while the cunning little veteran talked of how to play the game. Segura would draw diagrams on paper and show Jimmy what shots to make in certain situations. Then they would practice them the next day.

Tennis is a game of strategy as well as strength and speed. A smart player tries to maneuver an opponent out of position. If he can't hit the ball to a spot which an opponent cannot reach, the smart player tries to hit it so that the other person will have a difficult return. He also tries to make an opponent hit the shots which give him the most trouble. In either case, the opponent's weak return can be smashed out of reach.

"I try for a shot where, on the next ball, I'm going

to make my opponent eat it — sometimes literally," Connors has said.

That is one of the things he learned from Segura, who is called "Little Pancho" by tennis players. Gonzales, Jimmy's other teacher, is "Big Pancho." Gonzales is 6-feet, 3-inches tall. Segura is 5-feet, 7-inches tall and weighed 145 pounds in his playing days. But he won amateur championships after coming to the United States from Ecuador, where he was born in 1921. Then he became a professional and a teacher.

"When you're small," Segura has said, "you get power and speed by moving into the ball; you use the momentum of your body."

Connors is tireless on the court, running with his "nose to the ball" from start to finish of every match. When a player stays low with his knees bent, he can see the ball better, hit it sooner. But everyone has a tendency to straighten his knees and back as he becomes tired. Connors simply keeps himself in such good physical condition that he seldom tires. He runs a couple miles a day.

He also has exceptionally good vision, which helps him pick up the direction of a ball as soon as his opponent strikes it.

"He looks like he's moving toward where you're

going to hit the ball before you hit it." Bob Carpenter, an Australian player, has said. "He lunges over with that funny backhand and hits a screamer just this far over the net and that far inside the line. I used to think he was just lucky, but it's not that at all. He's bloody brilliant, he is."

Big Pancho taught Jimmy about the power game. Even though Connors cannot play that style of tennis, he understands it very well. He knows what his bigger, stronger opponents want to do on the court. That is one of the reasons for his success.

While he was learning all of this, Jimmy was living the strangest life imaginable for a teenager from the Midwest. It was totally different from Belleville.

Each school morning, Jimmy would drive his car, a Corvette, to Rexford High School in Beverly Hills, where most of the students were children of wealthy and famous parents. The Connors family is not wealthy, but it is not poor, either. They could afford an expensive car and fine sports clothes for Jimmy.

Jimmy has never been interested in school work and he didn't have any more friends at the California school than in Belleville. Usually after his second class he would drive to a tennis club and begin practicing. Often he would play from 10:30 in the morning until 8:30 at night.

He met and played with the sons of movie and television stars like Dean Martin and Desi Arnaz. He went to the restaurants and clubs where the rich and famous relaxed and he was invited to their parties. But it didn't make much impression on Jimmy. Tennis was his whole life. He couldn't be bothered with anything that interfered with it. A friend who knew him then says that Jimmy had "an amazing hunger" for work, meaning tennis.

After high school, Jimmy enrolled at the University of California at Los Angeles (UCLA), but he was not a serious student. He remembers taking a couple of music courses with basketball star Bill Walton, but not much else about his college career.

He played tennis for UCLA and became the first freshman ever to win the national collegiate championship. However, competition at the college level is not very stiff compared to the play of the better professionals. Connors' title didn't impress the world-class tennis players.

But Jimmy also played in non-college tournaments and he began to attract attention. A few days after his 18th birthday, he reached the finals of the Pacific Southwest Tournament, an "open" event, meaning that both professional and amateur players could enter. The amateurs could not accept prizes, however. Jimmy played one of his teachers, Gonzales, in the finals and lost to him.

Gonzales told other players that young Connors was a coming champion, but not many took Gonzales seriously. They laughed at Jimmy's unorthodox two-handed backhand. They said that he would burn himself out with his furious attacking style. Players with big booming serves would overwhelm Connors, the critics said.

But Gonzales and Little Pancho Segura could see into the future. They could tell that their student's game was taking shape. He was perfecting his natural talents.

During the next year, 1971, Jimmy reached the finals of five tournaments, including the important Pacific Southwest, where once again he lost to Gonzales. If he had been a professional, he would have won $50,000 in prize money that year. His game was getting better in every way. He was confident that he could hold his own with the world's top players.

Early in the year 1972, Jimmy telephoned his parents and told them that he had decided to become a professional. He was still 19, but he had been preparing for this day all of his life.

"I loved it all," Jimmy told an interviewer from Sports Illustrated magazine. "People have criticized my mom for trying to make me what she wasn't, but . . . this is what I've always wanted to be."

Connors won the first two tournaments he entered as a professional and five more his first year. He began cutting down the giants of the game, people like Stan Smith, the 6-foot, 5-inch American star.

"The problem of playing someone like Connors," Smith said, "is the constant pressure. You know that if you hit any sort of weak shot, he's going to attack it."

The best known tennis tournament in the world is played at Wimbledon, England, each July. Wimbledon is to tennis what the World Series is to baseball and the Super Bowl to professional football. Players would rather win a Wimbledon championship than any other, even though they might collect three times as much prize money in another tournament.

Connors's first Wimbledon tournament was in 1972 and he did very well. He upset South Africa's Bob Hewitt, another giant both in stature and ability, before losing to

Ilie Nastase, the Rumanian star who was soon to become the world's No. 1-ranked player.

Connors fell in love that same summer. He had met Chris Evert a couple of years earlier, but hadn't really noticed her. Then a week or two before Wimbledon began, they met again in England. They were immediately attracted to each other.

Chris, two years younger than Jimmy, was the rising star of women's tennis. Shy off the court, she was a picture of cool concentration when playing. She was, in fact, just the opposite of Connors, who can be bubbling with jokes one day and brooding over his problems the next.

It was a lonely time for Connors. He was traveling by himself all over Europe and the United States. His grandmother, whom he loved very much, had died suddenly. His own mother, always his best fan and greatest friend, could not spend much time with him.

Chris, too, felt the pressure of being a celebrity while still in her teens. She was sought after for interviews and by fans. Like Jimmy, she had to cope with those pressures while playing older, stronger, more experienced opponents.

Together, the two found their burdens lighter. Chris steadied Jimmy. He helped her overcome her shyness and acquire self-confidence. They practiced together and had fun doing things neither had previously taken time to do. They went dancing and sight-seeing.

After Wimbledon, where Chris lost in the semifinals to Evonne Goolagong, each visited the other's family. They had much in common. Both fathers had attended Notre Dame. Like Jimmy's mother, Chris's father was once a professional player and now is a respected instructor in Fort Lauderdale, Florida. Chris learned from him, as Jimmy did from his mother.

The young tennis stars became engaged and once planned to marry in November 1974. After deciding to postpone the marriage, it appeared early in 1975 that the romance had cooled. Chris had told reporters that there were no longer any plans for a wedding. She said she intended to concentrate on her tennis and was sure Jimmy would do the same.

This breakup was well in the future in 1972 when Connors won 75 tournament matches, more than any other United States man. But he was ranked only third in the country and many tennis players and fans still believed that he would never be No. 1.

One reason given was that Connors played mainly on the United States Lawn Tennis Association's (USLTA) winter indoor tour. Almost all of the other top professionals played the World Championship Tennis (WCT) tour.

Bill Riordan, Connors's business advisor, also manages the USLTA tour. Connors has said that he prefers it because he does not want to commit himself to play as many tournaments as the WCT requires.

Riordan has pointed out that Connors meets all of the other top players many times at the major summer tournaments all over the world. Nevertheless, it is likely that Connors eventually will play on the WCT tour, if only to quiet his critics. Late in 1974, Australian Superstar John Newcombe charged Connors with dodging him on the tournament trail.

For all these reasons, Connors was still better known in the spring of 1973 as Chris Evert's boy friend than for his own great playing ability. Connors lost in the early rounds of the Italian and French Open Tournaments that spring and then was beaten badly at Wimbledon. His critics began to say he would always be a second-rate player.

Then whammo! Connors turned the tennis world upside down.

He entered the U.S. Professional Championship Tournament at Boston just a couple of weeks after failing at Wimbledon. His first opponent was towering Stan Smith, co-ranked with Connors as the top player in the United

States. Connors blew Smith off the court. Then he beat Ray Moore, Dick Stockton, Cliff Richey — all world-class players — and, finally, defeated Arthur Ashe, who had won the tournament twice before.

"He just kept hitting the ball harder and harder, deeper and deeper," said Ashe. "I've never played anyone who could keep up such tremendous groundstrokes for so long. He's extremely smart, not very conventional. He does the opposite of what you expect."

Groundstrokes are those hit after the ball has bounced on the court. Connors was hitting them like a machine gun, backhanded and forehanded, to one corner and then to the other. He would keep an opponent running back and forth until he could angle a shot past him or force a weak return. Then Connors would charge the net to smash it back for a point.

"That was the most pleasureful week I've ever had," Connors told a writer for the New York Times. "They said I couldn't play the big boys . . . I'd had it up to here."

It was at that tournament where Connors's style of play was finally recognized. He doesn't overpower his opponents; he wears them down. "The big hitters are easy meat," he has said. "I can destroy them."

The argument against the two-handed backhand is that it shortens the reach, but Connors is so quick and his

coordination so splendid that he overcomes any loss of reach. Incidentally, Chris Evert also uses both hands and she like Connors, is deadly accurate.

But Chris very seldom takes a risk. She stays back at the baseline, the end of the court, and keeps the ball in play while she waits for her opponent to make a mistake.

Connors is a gambler, a reckless, daredevil competitor. He will charge an opponent's return, risking everything on his own judgment of where the ball will be hit. Usually he is right. His excellent eyesight and quick hands and the endless hours of study under "Little Pancho" have made him an expert.

"Jimmy has great ball sense," Segura has said. "He knows where it's coming off the other guy's racket because he knows what spin and pace he's put on the ball himself. Jimmy doesn't think anymore; he reacts automatically."

This ability to react instinctively and instantly is the mark of all great athletes when they're playing at their best.

Another feature of Connors's style is his ability to produce winning shots from the brink of disaster. Time after time at crucial moments he has flung his body sideways in the air to reach a ball that appeared to be beyond him.

The only player who consistently has given Connors trouble is Ilie Nastase, his best friend among the players. "I just can't seem to tell where the ball is going," Connors said once, adding with a grin, "Of course, he can't either."

The astonishing victory at Boston was the beginning of a year-long winning spree by Connors. During the next nine months, he entered 19 major tournaments, won 12 of them and advanced at least to the semifinals in 5 others.

In an era when dozens of tremendously talented players are competing, Connors's string of victories is almost unbelievable. It established him as a genuine superstar, a man who will be a major force in tennis for years to come, according to promoter Jack Kramer, once a great player himself.

Connors won $146,400 in prize money in 1973. Then he took a break from tournament play and made another $100,000 playing for Baltimore of the new World Team Tennis league. In addition to that, he made an estimated $50,000 for endorsements and personal appearances. Although he was just 21 years old, it was estimated that Connors already had earned more than half a million dollars from tennis.

He also had made some enemies. Undoubtedly some people resent or envy him because he has been so successful. But Connors also is criticized for his tactics on the court. He will bounce the ball a dozen or more times before serving. The delay may irritate the man across the net. He will blow endlessly on his fingers to dry them while his opponent

fidgets. He will argue with officials and with fans if he dislikes decisions or remarks from the gallery.

Ask him why he behaves that way and he'll say all players have their own habits which may irritate their opponents. A match is like a war, he said once. Players are struggling to maintain concentration and the least little thing will set off a temper explosion.

The things he does also help him concentrate, Connors says, adding: "My methods are just different from theirs. They don't bother me. Why should what I do bother them?"

"Nuts," say his opponents, "he does it to distract us."

Like him or not, tennis people are going to have to put up with Connors for a long time.

Returning to London, Connors breezed through Wimbledon in 1974, easily defeating the veteran Ken Rosewall for the men's singles title. Meanwhile, Chris Evert was winning the Wimbledon women's singles title.

The young couple danced at the Wimbledon Victory Ball, then returned to the United States where Connors won the United States Open at Forest Hills in New York City, this country's most important tournament. Again he met Rosewall in the finals and again Jimmy won easily. Actually, he routed, even destroyed Rosewall in this match.

After Forest Hills, tennis fans began wondering just how good Connors was. By the end of 1974, Connors was alone at the top of the U.S. rankings. He was also the top money winner among the touring pros, winning $285,490 in 1974. Fans were asking how Connors would compare with the all-time great players.

Will Grimsley, Associated Press sports writer who has seen most of the finest players, offered this reply:

"The answer can only be provided by time and future performances, but on the basis of his performances this year at Wimbledon and later at Forest Hills, no one can deny that for those quick, exciting, unbelievable moments at least, Jimmy Connors was the best tennis player who ever lived."

Jimmy's friend Pancho Gonzales was known as a "Killer" on the court. But none of the game's giants, Grimsley said, "ever played the relentlessly murderous tennis that Connors unleashed . . . against the great Rosewall."

Although he was 39, Rosewall was a physical marvel, Grimsley noted. And before meeting Connors, Rosewall had played and defeated such players as John Newcombe, judged by many to be the best player in the world, and Stan Smith. Rosewall, one of the great players of all time, clearly was at the peak of his game.

Yet Connors overwhelmed Rosewall. Twice.

"The kid is fantastic," said Little Pancho Segura. "There will never be another like him."

JACKIE ROBINSON
MUHAMMAD ALI
O. J. SIMPSON
JOHNNY BENCH
WILT CHAMBERLAIN
ARNOLD PALMER
A. J. FOYT
JOHNNY UNITAS
GORDIE HOWE
WALT FRAZIER
PHIL AND TONY ESPOSITO
BOB GRIESE

JACK NICKLAUS
BILL RUSSELL
MARK SPITZ
VINCE LOMBARDI
BILLIE JEAN KING
ROBERTO CLEMENTE
JOE NAMATH
BOBBY HULL
HANK AARON
JERRY WEST
TOM SEAVER

superstars!
superstars!
superstars!
superstars!

CREATIVE EDUCATION SPORTS SUPERSTARS

FRANK ROBINSON
PANCHO GONZALES
LEE TREVINO
KAREEM ABDUL JABBAR
JEAN CLAUDE KILLY
EVONNE GOOLAGONG
ARTHUR ASHE
SECRETARIAT
ROGER STAUBACH
FRAN TARKENTON
BOBBY ORR
LARRY CSONKA

BILL WALTON
ALAN PAGE
PEGGY FLEMING
OLGA KORBUT
DON SCHULA
MICKEY MANTLE
EVEL KNIEVEL
JIMMY CONNORS
CHRIS EVERT
PETER REVSON
KATHY WHITWORTH
JACKIE STEWART